Francis Seymour Haden

Earth to Earth

A Plea for a Change of System in our Burial of the Dead

Francis Seymour Haden

Earth to Earth
A Plea for a Change of System in our Burial of the Dead

ISBN/EAN: 9783337118464

Printed in Europe, USA, Canada, Australia, Japan

Cover: Foto ©Andreas Hilbeck / pixelio.de

More available books at **www.hansebooks.com**

EARTH TO EARTH.

*A PLEA FOR A CHANGE OF SYSTEM IN
OUR BURIAL OF THE DEAD.*

BY

FRANCIS SEYMOUR HADEN, F.R.C S.

" *Lay her i' the earth.*"

London :

MACMILLAN AND CO

1875.

[*Reprinted, by Permission, from the Times.*]

PREFACE.

THE three letters which are here reprinted embody a long-contemplated effort to expose and remedy a great social evil.

The attempt of a small portion of the press to diminish their influence by ignoring the character of this effort and by affecting to consider and treat them from an æsthetical point of view, will deceive but few.

The prompt demand for their republication satisfies their author that the common-sense of the majority is with him, and that neither his letters nor the sanitary purpose he has had in writing them are in any danger of being misunderstood.

June 23.

EARTH TO EARTH.

TO THE EDITOR OF "THE TIMES."

SIR,—An agitation, attributable possibly to an imperfect appreciation of the merits of the case, has been caused by the proposal of certain German and Italian writers in their own country, and of an eminent surgeon in this, to substitute the burning of the dead for their interment.

Interment, the apostles of Cremation tell us, in substance if not in terms, and speaking of it in its most comprehensive sense, is repulsive in idea, costly and ineffectual in fact, horrible in practice, a vilification of the dead, and a danger to the living. In a variety of publications which have excited much attention, they denounce not any particular mode of interment, or any palpable abuses which they recognise as having crept into the practice to discredit it, but the practice itself. They take no notice of the fact that the dead are little more than nominally buried, and that, by the interposition between them and the earth that should resolve them of such media as wood, lead, brick, and the like, interment as a principle is rendered all but nugatory, and as a practice deprived of its *raison d'être*. Finally they leave it to be inferred, since they give us no hint to the contrary, that the evils thus created are inherent in the principle of interment, and upon this inference, and upon no other ground, found their recommendation of Cremation.

It is the object of this letter, Sir, not so much to join issue with the Cremationists whose position I must venture to think untenable, as to invite attention to the important fact which underlies, and to some extent excuses, their proposals,— viz., the fact that the dead are improperly buried; and, with reference to the serious and pressing evils which have resulted from our present mode of interment, to suggest a consideration of the following propositions :—

1. That the natural destination of all organized bodies that have lived, and that die on the earth's surface, is the earth.

2. That the evils which they (the Cremationists) would have us believe to be inseparable

from the principle of interment are independent of that principle, and wholly of our own creation.

3. That the source of these evils is to be found, not in the burial of the dead, but in the unreasoning sentiment which prompts us to keep them unburied as long as possible, and then to bury them in such a way that the earth can have no access to them.

4. That the burial of the body supposes its resolution by the direct agency of the earth to which we commit it, and that the earth is fully competent to effect that resolution.

5. That to seek to prevent the beneficent agency of the earth by inclosing the dead in hermetically sealed coffins, brick graves, and vaults, is in the highest degree unphilosophical, since it engages us in a vain resistance to an inevitable dispensation, and has led us to accumulate in our midst a vast store of human remains in every stage and condition of decay.

6. That the remedy for such evils is not in Cremation but in a sensible recognition of, and a timely submission to, a well-defined law of nature, and in legislative action to enforce the provisions of that law.

The claim that the earth has upon its dead, no less than that which the dead have upon the earth, is a proposition, one would have thought, too obvious to merit discussion. To understand it we need only consider the properties with which the soil at our feet and everywhere at our disposal has been endowed ; that it is the most potent disinfectant known and the readiest of application, and that, by a combination of forces inherent in it which might well appear contradictory but for the wonderful purposes they are destined to effect, it is resolvent and re-formative as well; that that which under the influence of the air was putrefaction, in the earth is resolution ; that which was offensive becomes inoffensive ; that which was mere decay a process of transformation. To question the competency of the earth, thus endowed, to effect the resolution and conversion of its dead, or to fail to perceive and profit by that competency, would pass comprehension if habit had not taught us to shut our eyes to it, and if the advocates of Cremation had not stepped in to tell us that we may improve upon it.

The main conditions of effective and of non-effective burial are shortly these. When the body dies, putrefaction sets in at once, and, for as long as it is allowed to remain exposed to the air, continues. The air excluded, the process is arrested ; the air readmitted, the process goes on. If the body have been dead some days, and putrefaction be well advanced before the adoption of measures to protect it from the influence of the air, the process will be arrested at the point it has then attained, and, for as long as the physical conditions are permitted to last, will remain at that point. Two methods of excluding the air from a dead body present themselves in practice, the direct and natural method of placing it in the earth, and what may be called the evasive and unnatural method of inclosing it in an air-tight case or coffin. By adopting the first method, inasmuch as we both exclude the air and invoke the resolvent action of the earth, we fulfil all the conditions of effective burial. By adopting the second method we fulfil only one of these conditions, and, for the sake of keeping the body by us a few days longer than is safe or reasonable, prevent the other. In the first case resolution at once takes the place of putrefaction ; in the last the condition of putrefaction is rendered permanent. In the first case if we look for that body at the end of five or six years we shall not find it, or, rather, we shall only find the inorganic part of it—the organic, resolved into its constituent elements, having re-entered the atmosphere. In the last, if we look for it after fifty years, we shall find it as we left it—*plus* the action upon it of the air and of the fluids of the body which we have included with it in the coffin—that is to say, in a state of advanced but unprogressive putrefaction.

The following illustrations represent aptly enough the two conditions described :—

On Christmas Day, 1870, I buried in a corner of my garden a favourite dog. On the 1st of November, 1874—the other day—I dug down upon the spot and recovered all that was recoverable of the body of my old companion. The residue lies upon a sheet of white foolscap paper on the table before me. It consists of a few scattered bones with a little friable matter loosely attached to them which has all the physical characters of common earth, without the slightest odour or anything to indicate that it had once been animal tissue. Resolution, in fact, except as to the bones which have lost much of their weight and the cancellous structure of which is beginning to break down, has been fully effected.

In 1868 I was permitted to visit the burial-ground of St. Andrew's, Holborn, then, with its contents, in course of removal to make way for the new Viaduct. The ground about the church had become raised 15ft. or 18ft. above its original level, and perpendicular sections had been made in it, here and there, from its surface to a depth varying from 10 feet to 30 feet or more. The face of these sections represented the interments of three centuries and a half. All the burials, except those in the Plague-pit and one or two others to be presently mentioned, had been made in wooden or leaden coffins, some of which were still intact, and some broken in. Little difference as to condition could be perceived between the coffins of Charles II.'s time and those recently used, or between the coffins which were of lead and those which were of wood. In the coffins which were intact were their contents, also intact but putrid, unrecognizable. In those which had been broken in nothing was to be found but a little ordinary earth, corresponding chiefly to the extraneous matters which had accompanied the interment, and, occasionally, not always, a few bones. Nothing more. The body itself had disappeared, and "earth to earth" had been accomplished. Here and there, in other parts of the ground, were graves lined with brick and filled with water in which the coffins of those who had been buried in peculiar honour still floated, some head, some feet uppermost, as their gaseous contents determined. Here, again, a few fetters indicated the spot where some evil-doer had undergone what was intended, no doubt, to be the last sentence of degradation, but whose poor body, having had the advantage of being buried without a coffin, had disappeared—as had also, for the same reason, the tenants of the Plague-pit. The whole tangible remaining mass, consisting of several thousand bodies, was removed, night by night to Ilford, where it now lies in a pleasant garden, and the new Rectory House of St. Andrew's stands upon the restored level. The removal was effected without difficulty, danger, or scandal, and a letter somewhat similar to the present one, which I wrote to you at the time, was not printed for fear of the embarrassment it might occasion while the ghastly work was in progress.

These illustrations will now help us to realise the following facts :—

That the condition of these unresolved dead is precisely the condition to which all are condemned who have been kept unburied for a week, and then are buried in closed coffins.

That this dead population — these festering tenants-in-perpetuity of the soil—outnumber by hundreds of thousands the living population above them, and that unless (as in the case with the Holborn burial ground) an Act of Parliament should interpose to remove them, there they must lie incapable of further change, a reproach to our intelligence and a source of poison to the soil, for any time to come.

That, unwarned and undeterred by the magnitude of the evils we have thus created, we are still engaged in extending and perpetuating them in cemeteries so close to town that they must soon become a part of it.

That were the dead only properly buried not one of these evils would have any existence—not a single dead body would remain to infect the soil—and a quantity of land of incalculable value, now hopelessly alienated, would be liberated for purposes of hygiene or of utility.

And what, after all, it is now time to ask, is the

nature of the advantage that we are content to
purchase at this heavy cost, and to obtain which we
do not hesitate to deprive the dead of their sole
prerogative ? Simply, and solely, the satisfaction
of keeping them unburied a few days longer than
Nature intended ! The body that should have
been laid in the ground three days ago still lies
up stairs, a sheet drawn over the face to protect it
from the flies, and the windows slightly opened to
relieve the upper part of the house of the sick-
ening *aura* that has begun to pervade it. No
one that could help it has gone into the room
these three days, and they that have had to pass the
door have passed it hurriedly and furtively. Then,
when from its condition the body can no longer be
allowed to remain exposed, and when, in reason, its
interment should be effected, comes instead the
stereotyped announcement that the "closure of
the coffin can be no longer delayed," and then
three, or even four more, miserable, fretful, useless
days follow. You cannot go out—it would not be
decent ; you cannot sleep because you cannot go
out ; your waking hours are passed in a forced
and irritating inactivity, your nights in painful
endeavours to realize the cherished lineaments
which, by an evasion of Nature's plan, you are

still able to keep within a few feet of you—not, indeed, as you saw them when summoned to look upon them for the last time before they were 'screwed down," but as they were a week before—beautiful with the peculiar beauty that distinguishes the recently dead, and the impression of which you would have been only too glad to be able to retain. At length the shuffling of many feet upon the stairs, and the dull shocks sustained by the walls in the descent of the heavy coffin, tell you that the time has come when custom has decreed that you may be released, and the dead put to its rest. And what a rest! Surely, Sir, it is time that, by a mere effort of our common sense and moral courage, we put an end to so irrational a practice and opened our eyes to the fact that we cannot thus outrage a Divine ordinance with impunity; that whenever it may please us to bury our dead properly—and nothing is easier—Earth will be found competent to do her own work, and Nature to carry out her own laws: and that a recourse to Cremation, or to any other proceeding involving a departure from those laws, will turn out to be quite unnecessary.

How, then, are we to bury our dead? Clearly

within a reasonable time of their dissolution, and in coffins (if we must have coffins) of such a construction as will not prevent their resolution. No coffin at all would, of course, be best, or a coffin of the thinnest substance which would not long resist the action of the earth, or a coffin the top and sides of which admitted of removal after the body had been lowered into the grave, or a coffin of some light permeable material, such as wicker or lattice-work, open at the top, and filled in with any fragrant herbaceous matters that happened to be most readily obtainable. A layer of ferns or mosses for a bed, a bundle of sweet herbs for a pillow, and as much as it would still contain after the body had been gently laid in it of any aromatic or flowering plant for a coverlet—such a covering, in short, as, while it protected the body from the immediate pressure of the earth as effectually as the stoutest oak, would yet not prevent its resolution. I can conceive no better form of coffin. Let us emulate, too, the healthy sentiment of those older Jews who considered it an indignity and an injury to be refused prompt burial and so made an offence to the living, and bury it while it is still grateful to every sense, and while,—if we feel it an effort and a sacrifice to part with it,—

we may also feel that we are making that effort and submitting to that sacrifice in the cause of the dead.

Nor would there be the least difficulty in framing an Act which, with a truer consideration for the dead, should provide for such a mode of burying them as our reason and our interest require. The appointment in each district of a proper officer to take cognizance of everything relating to the dead of that district, should be one of the things such an Act provided for. An obligation on the part of every householder to report within a certain time the occurrence of any death or deaths under his roof should be another. The visit of such officer (also within a specified time) to verify the fact of death and to define and prescribe the requirements of the law as to time and mode of interment, another. And,—since it is our unnatural delay in burying the dead which necessitates their hermetic inclosure,—that the interval between death and inhumation should in no case exceed, say, 36, or at most 40, hours. The abolition of the permanent tenure of the ground by the dead and of the use of imperishable coffins, brick graves, vaults, and every impediment to the resolution of the

B

body should be another. The institution of special
Boards, corresponding to the Bureaux des Pompes
Funèbres in France, for the management of cemeteries (which Boards should not include the local
guardians of the poor, but which should be under
the direct supervision of the Board of Works)
another. And, in respect to the economy of the
ground, careful provision, of course, that graves
once used should not be reopened till ample
time had been given for the resolution of their
contents.

Nor, since it may be taken as an axiom that
Nature will ever be found ready to supply us with
the means of doing that which she requires us to
do, need we ever be at a loss for ground in which
to bury our dead. If it be true that a body, properly buried, is resolved in five, or, at most, six
years, it follows that, at that interval or at intervals
as much longer as we please, we may bury again
and again in the same ground with no other effect
than to increase its substance and to raise its surface. Is there, however, no ground in the immediate neighbourhood of our city that would be
the better—I put the question parenthetically and
only to illustrate the peculiar fitness and reason of   .

the suggestion—for this increase and for being thus raised? The Cremationists will tell us that there is not, but is there the shadow of a foundation for such a statement? Along the course of our great river from London to the sea, for instance, have we not vast lowland tracts of rich alluvial soil deposited by its current, and capable of being drained, planted, and beautified, in which, with equal benefit to the land and to ourselves, we may bury our dead for centuries? If, as we have seen, the surface of the Holborn burial ground was raised 15 or 18 feet by the interments within it of three centuries, why should not the lowlands of Kent and Essex be gradually raised and reclaimed in the same way, and as much as possible of the valuable ground in and about the city now occupied as cemeteries be restored to better uses? What if it take us thousands instead of hundreds of years thus to reclaim and elevate such lands, deprive them of their malarious character, and at the same time practically dispose of our difficulties as to burial for ever? With the broad and silent river for our Appian Way, and the salt breeze from the sea to refresh it and to swell the many-coloured sails which as long as we remain a nation will continue to tra- verse and enliven it, what better, more natural,

or more characteristic burial-place can a maritime
people have ?

And now, Sir, with the soil at our feet asking us
to reclaim and replenish her in this simple and
obvious way, what are we to think of the wild
project to drive into vapour the bodies of the 3,000
people that die weekly in greater London alone, at
a needless cost, an infinite waste, and (on such a
scale) with an effect on the respirable air of the
city that has yet to be estimated ? I say advisedly
"at an infinite waste," because it is incorrect to say
that, in its ultimate reception of the products of
Cremation, the earth acquires an augmentation of
its concrete substance equal to that which it
receives when a body is actually committed to
it. If that were so we might as well intercept and
burn up all the organic matter which has died, and
which in the course of nature would find its way
back to the earth. What really happens is this.
When the body, consisting as it does of organic
and of inorganic constituents in certain proportions, is placed within the earth, the organic
matters are dissipated by gaseous resolution,
by evaporation, and by the requirements of vege-
tation, while the inorganic remain to constitute

a portion, however small, of new earth. Exposed to the more rapid desiccation of the furnace something like the same thing, indeed, may
be said to result, since the fluids are driven off
and the solids remain ; but there is this essential
difference in the two processes—a difference fatal
to cremation—viz., that while, by the earth, the
solid residuum is wholly resolved and disposed of,
by the furnace it is left upon our hands; that
while one process, in short, is perfect and final,
the other is incomplete.   What are we to do
with this residuum, with this six, eight, or ten
pounds of solid matter (about the average weight,
by the way, of the Egyptian mummy) that the
furnace is incapable of driving off ?   Are we
to scatter it 'broadcast over our fields,' as re-
commended by a distinguished Cremationist?
Apart from the fact that this is only another
and a clumsy way of burying it I doubt a
general acquiescence in such a mode of disposing
of it, and rather fear that the tendency may be to
preserve it and that room must be found some-
where for the 3,000 urns or other vessels capable of
receiving it.   What are we to do with these urns ?
Are we to reopen our church vaults (happily closed
though still uncleansed) for their reception, or take

them into our houses and move them with our furniture with every change of abode? How will our
sons' sons, who have lost all interest in us, feel disposed to treat them? Will it not come to pass
that, perplexed by such embarrassing possessions,
they will one day want to get rid of them, and
will there not then be some risk of their desecration? What if, after all, they should be compelled
to listen to the voice of nature and driven to
bury them?

If the positions sought to be established in
this letter are true—if burial be the natural and
necessary process I have asserted it to be—we
may be sure that sooner or later, evade or
misinterpret her as we may, Nature (whether in
our columbaria or our cemeteries) will make her-
self heard at last, and—by the penalties she
imposes upon us for our abuse of her gifts—
compel us not only to bury our dead, but to bury
them properly.

I am, &c., &c.

January 12, 1875.

LETTER THE SECOND.

In my letter of the 12th of January, prompted mainly by such considerations as might be expected to occur to a person of my profession, and such as I have since found had occurred to many,[1] I ventured to propound a principle and affirm a fact: the principle, that, in the order and economy of Nature, it is the office of the earth to remove from our sight and turn to our advantage every form of organic decay accruing to its surface—decay that would otherwise overwhelm us; the fact, that we virtually, though no doubt quite innocently, ignore that principle when we fail to avail ourselves of the signal benefits which its application confers upon us, and when we seek to exempt from the friendly operation of the earth the decaying bodies of our

---

[1] " The Reliquary," July, 1864; " The Medical Times and Gazette," July—August, 1873, &c.

dead. Pleading for the dead, and for their right to
participate in these benefits,—a right of which,
without due consideration as it seems to me we
deprive them,—I contrasted the offensive putrefaction of buried and of imperfectly buried animal
matter with its comparatively benign disintegration when simply committed to the ground, and
—finding a warrant for what I wrote in the well-
known faculty of the earth to change the organic into the inorganic, the noxious into the
innocuous—claimed for the ἠρεμακαῦσις which
attends proper burial that it might rather be
regarded as a process of transformation than
a form of decay. Continuing, too, the argument
in the spirit of an absolute belief in the suffi-
ciency and perfection of all natural processes
and in the danger that must attend any syste-
matic attempt to contravene them, I pointed out
that, by our contrivances for preventing the
necessary and salutary action of the earth upon
the bodies of the dead, we had brought upon
ourselves a penalty the onerous nature of which
we were already abundantly sensible of, but
which in time would certainly, as far as this and
other populous cities were concerned, acquire the
proportions and consequences of a plague.

In the letter which I address to you to-day I propose, with your permission, to reduce these general reflections and statements to a practical shape; to show how the thing that is manifestly wrong may be avoided, and the thing that is right done; and, finding occasion as I go on to consider with the attention and respect to which they are fully entitled the fears and objections of others, to do what I can to remove those fears and objections. I hope to be able to effect this:—

1. By such a further insistence on the competency and power of the earth as may satisfy those who still suppose that natural burial within it must poison both it and the springs which have their rise in it.

2. By such a consideration of the signs of death and of our means of observing and verifying them as . may reassure those who fear the effect of any change in our present practice of deferred interment.

3. By such an explanation of the treatment which the body should receive after death, and after various kinds of death, as may dispel all apprehensions of the spread of infection from the disuse of closed coffins; and by an account

of such a simple mode of burial as I would see take the place of our present unnatural plan.

4. By such an exposure of the abuses attending the management of our present cemeteries, and such observations on the defective state of the law in respect to the safe and proper burial of the dead as may engage the action of Parliament, and, I trust, bring about their amendment; and,

5. By such suggestions for the formation and regulation of one or more new burial-places to the East of London as may combine facility of access with security that a grave once occupied should not again be disturbed till ample time had been given for the complete disappearance of its contents.

1. It has been well observed that since the excreta of animals during life and their bodies after death must all pass through a process of decay, and in new forms re-enter the atmosphere, some provision must exist in the world by which such a vast mass of corruption as they represent may do so innocuously.[1] That provision, I have said, exists in the earth. Two distinct forms of decay do, in fact, occur in

[1] Lyon Playfair—"Address on Health." Glasgow, 1874.

nature—putrefaction, which is a change set up
between the particles of unburied matter by
the air and by water, (both more or less im-
pure) to which it is exposed, and by minute
organisms which float in the air, and which
obtain direct access to it; and *erimacausis*, which
is the scientific name for the effect brought
about by the indirect access to the buried body
through porous soils of the same air and the
same water, but winnowed of their putrescent
elements by filtration, and chymically trans-
formed by the force which is known as surface affinity—the first of these forms giving
rise to compounds offensive to the senses and
pernicious to the health, the last to carbonic
acid, water, and ammonia, the food of plants,
and, through the agency of those plants, the
ultimate purifiers of the air. Our aim should,
therefore, be, by the burial of the body, to imi-
tate this *erimacausis*—to promote and not to
oppose it; and the more since it can be easily
shown, by a comparison of the waste of matter
in the excretions with the known volume of
the soft parts of the living body, that transformation proceeds so rapidly that the whole of
those soft parts are dissipated and renewed,

not every seven years, as is traditionally supposed, but every six weeks; so that that which
is our body to-day, and which we are so sedu-
lous to preserve, was not our body six weeks
ago, and would not be our body six weeks
hence. To desire to preserve such a body at
all, I have ventured to call an unreasoning
sentiment; to preserve it for an indefinite time
in a poisonous and putrescent state may, I think,
be stigmatized, without extravagance or impropriety, as an offence against society.

Nor, contrary to popular belief, does the decaying body itself, when buried in a sufficient quantity of earth to resolve it, impart any impurity
whatever to the adjacent soil or to the other
elements around it, a fact which any one may
ascertain for himself by digging down upon the
body of an animal which has been buried, it
matters not how long or how short a time,
and finding, (as he will do if he proceed cau-
tiously) that the soil in contact with it has only
been affected by it to about the eighth of an
inch, and that, until this very last film of en-
veloping earth has been reached and removed,
no smell whatever has been emitted from the
excavation he is making. There have now

been standing in my garden since January last
three open flower-pots containing tainted meat
—the first with a mere sprinkling, the second
with an inch, and the third with about two
inchês of earth covering the meat. From none
of these pots, not even the first, have I or others
been able, at any time, to detect the slightest
smell, though the cats in the neighbourhood (on
whose independent testimony I counted) have,
owing to a heavy shower which displaced the
covering film of earth in the first pot, at last
found out the meat in that pot and removed it.

Nor, again, is the effect of the earth upon
fluids in a state of putrescence at all less remarkable than upon solids—filtration through a
few feet of common earth being sufficient to
deprive the foulest water of any amount of
animal or other putrid matter contained in it.
We need go no further for a proof of this
than to a certain pump in Bishopsgate Street,
which stands opposite the rails of the old churchyard there, and of which Mr. Simon, the distinguished Medical Officer of the Privy Council,
gives us the following interesting account :—

"The water from this well is perfectly bright, clear, and
even brilliant; it has an agreeable soft taste, and is much

esteemed by the inhabitants of the parish, though, as will
be seen by the subjoined analysis, it is an exceedingly hard
water, and unfit for all culinary and most domestic purposes. . . . (yielding carbonates of lime and magnesia,
sulphate of lime, chloride of sodium, nitrates of potash.
soda, magnesia, and ammonia, silica, and phosphate of lime ;
but of organic matter, none or scarcely a trace.) . . .
The quantity of nitrates in this water is very remarkable.
These salts are doubtless derived from the decomposition
of animal matter in the adjacent churchyard. Their presence, conjoined with the inconsiderable quantity of organic
matter which the water contains, illustrates in a very forcible
manner the power that the earth possesses of depriving the
water that percolates it of any animal matter it may hold
in solution ; and, moreover, shows in how complete and
rapid a manner the process is effected. In this case the
distance of the well from the churchyard is little more than
the breadth of the footpath, and yet this short extent of
intervening ground has, by virtue of the oxydizing power of
the earth, been sufficient wholly to decompose and render
inoffensive the liquid animal matter that has oozed from the
putrefying corpses in the churchyard."

What need, Sir, to say more of this friendly
earth, when 2,500 years ago a barbarian (as we
should not hesitate to call him) thus apostro-
phizes it ?—

"When I am dead, my children," says Cyrus the Elder, [1]
"do not enshrine my body in gold and silver, or any other
substance, but return it to the earth as speedily as possible ;
for what can be more desirable than to be mixed with the
earth which gives birth and nourishment to everything that

---

[1] Xenophon.—"Cyropædia," vii. 7.

is excellent and good? I have always borne an affection to man, and now it seems to me a happy thing to be incorporated with that (earth) which is (so) beneficial to man."

2. It has been observed with some surprise that, in my former letter, I said nothing of the possibility of mistaking the signs of death, and that I offered no guarantee that, in the event of a radical change in our practice, such a mistake should not arise. I had not, in truth, thought any such notice necessary. "I saw in a moment he was dead," is the natural and spontaneous exclamation of even an inexperienced person who finds himself suddenly, and for the first time, in the presence of an unexpected 'death. No necessity to make a prolonged scrutiny to be sure of the fact. Dressed as he is and sitting in his chair, with all the appliances of life and of recent occupation about him, there is, yet, that in the appearance of the man before him which tells the new-comer at once that he is dead; and he, terrified by what he sees, runs without delay to inform others of his discovery. True, there are persons in the world capable of going into that room and of coming out again, and even of occupying themselves about the dead man without perceiving anything unusual, and

without a notion that for the last ten minutes
they have been in the presence of death. But
then there are also those who never look at the
sky—who know that there is a sky, and, generally, that it is gray or blue, bright or sombre,
but who never observe it—never climb that Pelion
upon Ossa of cumulus and stratus and look over
their golden edges into the far countries beyond.
Such as these might, indeed, see Death without
recognizing him; but for these it is useless to
write. And if, when Death has come upon us
unawares, he may be thus easily recognized, by
how much the more may we be sure of his
presence when his coming has been anticipated,
looked for, possibly longed for! Who that has
watched the progress towards death—the wasting
illness, the successive phenomena of the sinking
process, the obliteration of function after function,
the gradual obscuration of sense (and, happily, of
sensibility, for death is never painful), the "approach of death," as it is called, and yet has
doubted it when it came—mistaken the absolute
and final character of the silence that succeeds
it—of the still more characteristic rigidity that
so rapidly follows it?

Still, even in the most obvious cases, the presence of death should always be certified, not only by those who have watched and can testify to its apparent occurrence, but by those who are competent to pronounce with certainty upon the fact; and this and all other matters in connexion with the safe and proper disposal of the dead should (since the well-being of the community is concerned in it) be, in my humble judgment, the subject of police regulation.

Apart, however, from purposes of mere utility or propriety, it is but kind and reasonable to treat with the utmost consideration the doubts of those the disorder of whose moral rather than of whose physical perceptions renders them at such a moment unable or unwilling to persuade themselves of a truth which is only too apparent to every one else, and who naturally desire some sign by which they may be sure that the existence they have hung upon has ceased for ever. Is there any such sign, any such certainty? Undoubtedly there is. As long as life lasts, as long as a spark of vitality remains, two functions must be going on—two great functions which cannot, even for a few minutes, be in abeyance —the functions of *circulation* and of *respiration*. With our present means of investigation is it

possible that one or other of these functions
should be in operation and we not know it, or
so suppressed as to baffle our recognition? That
is the question ; and the answer to it may be
given with the utmost confidence in the one
word, "impossible ;" that, whatever may have
been the case with the imperfect appliances and
information of a past age, such ignorance of the
phenomena essential to vitality is impossible now.
If this were the place in which I could usefully
discuss in detail a matter which, in the event of
a doubt arising, would necessarily be referred to
medical experience, I would discuss it. If any
good could come of a popular description of that
science of *auscultation* which we now employ with
so much effect every day, but which was unknown
when the horrifying events of which we read are
said to have occurred, and when "the apparent
absence of sensation and motion"[1] were the
accepted signs of death—I would describe it. If
I might hope to render intelligible to those who
have not made physiology their study the use
of the *stethoscope*, and the action of the *sphygmo-
graph*, and of those recent instruments of Marey
which count, measure, and register the movements

---

[1] "On the Disorder of Death." W. Whiter, 1819.

of respiration and of the circulation as surely and as accurately as the anemometer measures and records the force and velocity of the wind—I would attempt it. Plainly, however, any such attempt would be as out of place as it would be useless. Far better than any assurances of mine must be the important declaration which, by the consideration of six of our most distinguished living physicians and surgeons, I am permitted to append to this letter. I invite the most timid reader to weigh well and consider every word of that declaration, and to ask himself if the eminent and honourable men who have placed their names at the foot of it would have done so if the least shadow of a doubt of what they were attesting had rested on their minds.

But, it may be said, since we may not always be within reach of medical aid, can you give us no single and simple sign by which we ourselves may judge of the fact of death? Certainly. Most of us know that, under the ordinary conditions of diffused heat, inanimate objects, whatever their substance or nature, acquire what is called an *equilibrium of temperature*, while animate objects have and maintain a temperature

of their own—*i.e.*, that every piece of furniture
in a given room in which there is no fire and
which derives its heat from the general warmth
of the air, acquires the temperature of the air of
that room ; that a thermometer suspended from
the ceiling, or placed on the mantelpiece, the
table, the chair, or the bed, would register the
same number of degrees of heat. Well, then,
this being so, suppose a human body in that
room and on that bed which for twenty-four
hours has presented the usual characteristics of
death but in respect of which it is desired to
make assurance doubly sure. Can it be done ?
Yes. If that body be alive it will *not* be subject
to the law just described, but will have a temperature of its own—higher or lower, it may be,
than that of the furniture about it, but still *a
temperature of its own*. If dead, it *will* be
subject to the physical laws which govern the
inert and inanimate objects around it—the bed
on which it lies and the table which is beside it
—and a thermometer placed on one or the other
will be found to stand, and to remain at, *the
same point.*

3. We are now, then, in the presence of death.
What are we to do to prepare the body for its

burial? We know the horrors of the cemetery, we have seen and resented the mockeries of undertakerism, and have determined that the remains of him who but now was one of us shall be exposed to neither. We know that his body must be returned to that earth which gave it life; that it must complete the cycle of its pilgrimage, and that we must do nothing to disturb or rupture the harmony of that cycle. How are we to proceed? We are asked to do a new thing, the principle of which is that the dead may not be dishonoured or the living sacrificed. How are we to do that thing? We have to consider the treatment the body should receive immediately after death from ordinary as well as from extraordinary causes. Next, the manner of its burial. Ordinary causes are assumed to be those in which death has followed upon illness, accident, or the exhaustion of age; extraordinary causes, fevers and infectious and contagious diseases generally. Let us first assume an ordinary cause.

The body, as soon after death as may be, is to be sponged, the eyes are to be closed, the chin supported, the limbs composed, and the hands crossed upon the breast. Superfluous

bed-clothes together with the impedimenta and
rejectamenta of the sick room are to be removed,
and a window is to be opened a few inches both
at the top and at the bottom. The papers of
the deceased may then be examined, and, if these
contain nothing to forbid it, the first preparations
for the funeral may be made in the following
way. As a part of the ordinary stock-in-trade
of every turner, brushmaker, or basketmaker will
be found, nested one within the other and of
every form and dimensions, the necessary covering
or coffin; at every herbalist's or florist's, its garni-
ture. Both being light and portable may be
delivered at the house in an hour or two, and
the body may be at once laid in it and strewn
(except the face and hands, which should be left
exposed) with its evergreen covering. All this
may be done by the nurses or elder servants or
members of the family, and no stranger need be
admitted.

There is now ample time to consider arrange-
ments—for the visit of the physician or surgeon
charged to verify the fact of death—to telegraph
to friends—and to make final preparations for
the interment. In these, instead of passing the
interval in the fretful tedium of an enforced idle-

ness, each member of the family may take a part; the men in effecting and completing the out-door formalities ; the women in those gentler offices about the dead that more naturally devolve upon them. The gloomy room which, rendered hideous by the paraphernalia supplied by the undertaker they instinctively avoided before, they may now freely enter. If it be winter, fires may be lighted in it, light let in, and its comfort and habitability fully maintained. Let us not intrude on its privacy. The men are away on the business of the dead—on the duties which for that day and the next devolve upon them—the women are left ; the mother, the wife, the daughter, the stranger, even, that is within their gates. The dead is in their keeping. Simple flowers and pleasant memories suggest the grateful nature of their task. Who that knows them will doubt their pious employment ?

The morrow come, and everything prepared inside and out, the necessary agents for the interment will enter the house for the first time and the last, and remove the body in a suitable carriage either by railway or by water to its resting-place outside the city, one of the male representatives of the family in every case accom-

panying it. There need be no procession through
the streets—no opportunity for display—nothing
to elicit either the sympathy or the criticism of
the neighbourhood (both on such an occasion
equally out of place), but, arrived at the cemetery,
the body may wait in the mortuary chapel attached
to it those who are to be present at its interment.
These, having been informed of the death, will go
and return, as their desires, affections, or respect
for the dead impel them. The assembly will be
in the chapel and at the grave-side only, where
the mourners, men and women (for since there is
to be no public display, both may go), will find
the trellised coffin on its bier—garnished and
beautified by loving hands—awaiting them. Not
a word of our impressive burial service need be
omitted, though more may be said in the chapel
and less at the grave-side, and then all will be
over. There will be no reunion at the house of
death. The conventional feast will not be spread.
The formal reading of the will may be at the
office of the legal adviser of the family on a day
appointed for the purpose; and the inmates of
the house of mourning may return to it and be
allowed to remain undisturbed. Next day every
one will "to his business."

"But how," writes a very eminent physician, "would you deal with the body in the case of death from any disease of which the contagious poison is strong, subtle, and diffusive? I presume that you would have it inclosed as soon as possible after death, and that some expedient might be contrived for opening the box or coffin and allowing the access of earth to the body when it has been lowered to its final resting-place." Not so. It is an interesting and instructive fact—a fact strongly corroborative of the propriety of open interment—that such an inclosure of the infected body would neither be necessary nor right. In such a case the wicker basket, instead of herbs, would simply be filled with rather finely divided charcoal. Charcoal has the property of absorbing and retaining in the multiplicity of its cells a large quantity, a magazine, in fact, of oxygen. Nothing from within, —no mephitic vapours, poisons, or *contagia* of any kind—can pass through those cells into the outer air without being encountered and, in chymical language, burnt up by the oxygen within them. One thing, and but one thing, could render the proceeding abortive, and that would be to conduct the operation in a closed box or coffin;

then everything would fail. The porous charcoal, imprisoned and cut off from its constant supply of oxygen from without, would become saturated by the mephitic gases from within, and the coffin would soon become as much a source of infection as if the charcoal had not been placed in it at all. Mr. P. H. Holland bored holes in a closed coffin in which was a body thus surrounded by charcoal, and, by means of an aspirator, drew through the centre of it and examined afterwards the air which it had contained, and found that it was less charged with putrescent matter than the air of the room in which the experiment had been conducted—in fact, that it was chymically pure.

At this point, Sir, mindful of the great value of the space which you so courteously place at my disposal, no less than the patience of your readers, I will ask your permission to break off my letter, and to defer for a few days what it is still necessary to say of cemeteries and their abuses.

I am, &c., &c.

May 19, 1875.

DECLARATION REFERRED TO AT p. 35.

" The following question, arising out of an apprehension admitted to exist, lest a curtailment of the interval now allowed between death and burial might lead to the accident of interment before life were extinct, has been proposed to us by Mr. Seymour Haden :—

" 'As hospital physicians and surgeons of extended experience, has it ever occurred to you to see a case of so-called suspended animation or trance which, in your opinion, could be mistaken for death ; and do you think, the present state of our knowledge and resources considered, that the occurrence of such a case, or of such a mistake, can be regarded as possible ?'

" In reply to this question we desire to say that no case of the kind it suggests ever presented itself to any of us, and to express our confident belief that the dread of the possible occurrence of such a case is without support in the medical experience of this country ; and, further, that the signs of death are as certain after a few hours' suspension of the vital functions as they can be after many days.

" It would, we feel, be a matter of regret, and

an indication of a low state of public intelligence if the groundless fears to which our attention has been directed by Mr. Seymour Haden should hinder, for a moment, the adoption of an improvement in our social system, the importance of which cannot be overrated.

      " GEORGE BURROWS, M.D., *President of the Royal College of Physicians.*
      " WM. FERGUSSON.
      " WILLIAM W. GULL, M.D.
      " WILLIAM JENNER.
      " JAMES PAGET.
      " THOMAS WATSON, M.D.

"LONDON, *March* 13, 1875."

LETTER THE THIRD.

YOUR readers may remember that at the close of my letter of the 19th May we had buried our burthen, not in the crowded cemetery but in a place of our own choosing outside the city, where, secure against disturbance and desecration, it might remain while those beneficent changes were being perfected in it which, though the last, are by no means among the least of the privileges accorded to its humanity.

4. To-day, in continuation of that letter, we must go back to one or other of our existing Metropolitan cemeteries, and, from the point of view of its pretensions to fulfil the hygienic purposes for which it was established, consider it in reference to the evils which arise either, directly, out of its defective constitution and management, or, indirectly, out of its connexions and trade interests, which are not

the interests of the public. The chief of these evils are :—

(*a*) The prevention of the resolution of the body by the use of the closed coffin, vault, and catacomb.

(*b*) The saturation and pollution of the soil by the piling together of a number of coffins in the same grave.

(*c*) The unfitness of the present cemetery for all the essential purposes of sepulture arising out of an improper selection of its geological site, and its dangerous proximity to the town ; and

(*d*) The influence in its councils, in a sense adverse to the interests of the public, of its chief proprietor, and virtual director, the undertaker.

(*a*) Since the coffin is the *fons et origo mali*, the tangible and material agent in the production of all the evils which it is the object of these letters to remedy, the necessary considerations attaching to it should have precedence of other matter, and we should try to ascertain at starting whether its first use was suggested by fashion or dictated by necessity. That, at all times, it was looked upon as a questionable contrivance may be inferred from

the occasional requests of sensible persons to be
buried without it, and from the earliest records of
our cathedrals and parish churches which provide
for the payment of larger fees for those buried in
coffins than for those buried without—for " chested
than for unchested buryalls "—but chiefly from the
elaborate judgments which, from time to time, have
been delivered in condemnation of its use and of
the indefinite tenure of the soil which that use
implies. Lord Stowell says[1] :—

" It has been argued that the ground once given to the
body is appropriated to it for ever ; that it is literally in
mortmain unalienably ; that it is not only the *domus ultima*,
but the *domus æterna* of that tenant, who is never to be disturbed, be his condition what it may. The introduction of
another body into that lodgment at any time, however
distant, is an unwarrantable intrusion. . . . In support
of these positions it seems to be assumed that the tenant
himself is imperishable ; for, surely there can be no inextin-
guishable title, no perpetuity of possession, belonging to a
subject which itself is perishable. But the fact is that
' man ' and ' for ever ' are terms quite incompatible in any
state of his existence, dead or living, in this world. The
time must come when *ipse periere ruinæ*, when the post-
humous remains must mingle with and compose a part of
that soil in which they have been deposited. . . . The
domus æterna is a mere flourish of rhetoric ; the process of
nature will speedily resolve them into an intimate mixture

---

[1] " Gilbert v. Buzzard." Haggard's Reports.

with their kindred dust ; and their dust will help to furnish
a place of repose for other occupants in succession.   The
common cemetery is not *res unius ætatis*, the property of one
generation now departed, but is likewise the common
property of the living, and of generations yet unborn . .
. . Any contrivance, therefore, which prolongs the time of
dissolution beyond the period at which the common local
understanding and usage have fixed it is an act of injustice.
since by such contrivances it is, in course of time, given to a
comparatively small number of dead to shoulder out the
living and their posterity. . . . Coffins are not recognized by any authority whatever ; mention of them is no-
where made, but rather studiously avoided in the Burial
Service of the Church of England, and, generally, their use
can only be regarded as an encroachment on the rights of
the living."

Coffins, it is not disputed, have been in use for
all time. Joseph " dieth and is chested," in Egypt ;
but a hundred and eighty years ago, coffins, though
in use, were not in common use in England, the
plainer sort of us being content before that time to
be carried to our graves in open chests or coffers
which were kept at the parish church for the occasion, and only employed to convey the body from
the house of death to that other house which " hath
been appointed for all living," after which they
were returned to their accustomed place of deposit,
which was usually a niche in the church wall.   Arrived at the grave (" when they come to the grave,

while the corpse is made ready to be laid *into* the earth ") the body, properly enveloped, at one time in coarse linen kept together by bone pins, and later in woollen, was removed from its temporary case and buried ; the old Ritualist, Wheatley, making this removal from its coffin and " it's just a-going to be put into the ground " (" we therefore commit his body to the ground ") the occasion for a homily on the shortness and misery of temporal life and on our entire dependence at the last on the help and mercy of God.[1] This open burial, again, permitted a registration of the fact by the Vicar that it had been " made in woollen," according to the Act. Still earlier a couple of planks, separated at the head and foot by a turf, were used for the same purpose of carriage, and these, since they in no way retarded the resolution of the body, were often buried with it.[2] When and why did these poor planks assume the form and every-day use of the present coffin ? I have searched in vain for an answer, reasonable or unreasonable, to this question. In the time of the Plague ? To avert infection ? Happily, no ; for in that emergency no time was

[1] " The Reliquary," No. 17, 1864.

[2] " Antiquities of Myddle." Gough. 1700.

given for the perfection of a contrivance which
might at any time have subjected us to a renewal
of its outbreak. When, then? Apparently, when
the pretension which attends the acquisition of
wealth without intelligence suggested its use ;
when it was desired to keep the body for days for
the purpose of giving it an ostentatious funeral ;
when the prosperous hosier or vintner aspired to
the fashions and follies of his betters ; when time
was needed, not to honour the dead, but to open
the pestilent vault and prepare the " obsequious "
mourning ; when, in the jargon of the undertaker,
in short (the covert irony of which it was not given
to him to understand), funerals came to be " per-
formed" in this country, and when a week was
wanted to arrange the pageant which was to set
out with the blazon of a mock heraldry, and to
return with a dozen of the performers dangling
their legs from the but now vacated hearse. If,
Sir, while illustrating an important hygienic
principle, and anxious to render that principle
intelligible and to prove it practicable, I permitted
myself to describe a ceremonial in marked con-
trast with this the details of which have seemed to
some superfluous, it may not be amiss to say that,
by others, those very details have been deemed

desirable and even indispensable. Meanwhile, the more lenient critic—seeing that the Greek word κοφίνος is properly translated "a twig basket, or pannier," and that Wycliffe's rendering of καὶ ἦραν τὸ περισσεῦον τῶν κλασμάτων δώδεκα κοφίνους πλήρεις is, "and thei token ye relifis of broken gobetis, twelve cofyns ful [1]"—will admit that my suggestions, however trite, have not been unauthorized.

I need not occupy your space, Sir, by a description in detail of the basket coffin, since all the models which I have had made of it, and which have been obligingly made for me by others, are, by the courtesy of the Duke of Sutherland, now collected at Stafford-house, and since I am permitted by the Duke to say that on Thursday, the 17th, and on Saturday the 19th inst., they may be seen there, from four to six o'clock, by any lady or gentleman on presentation of an ordinary visiting card. By this opportune and public-spirited initiative on the part of his Grace a measure of the practical usefulness of these baskets may be obtained, and possible suggestions for their improvement elicited. My object being the establishment of a principle, I need scarcely say that I am not

[1] St. Matthew xiv. 20.

wedded to their use, and that if anything can be
devised lighter, stronger, and more portable ; as
inexpensive and suitable for the carriage of the
body to the grave, and for promoting its resolution
when there ; as well as for encaging and keeping
together the bones after the disappearance of the
soft parts (for the wicker basket will long outlast
its tenant), I shall see its introduction with pleasure
and be the first to propose its substitution for my
simple contrivance.

Two things in reference to coffins yet remain to
be said ; one is that any form of solid wood is
unfit for their construction ; the other that the
introduction of the open coffin, whatever its
material, will necessitate, for the mere purpose of
carriage to the grave, a return to the employment
of the old English hearse or pall-canopy, a fine
example of which covers the remains of the Earl
of Warwick in the Beauchamp Chapel.[1] Wood, in
moist earth, is nearly indestructible. The modest
planks of our forefathers are found as they were
buried centuries ago,[2] and wooden coffins of
Charles II.'s time were removed from the Holborn

---

[1] " English Church Furniture." H. Peacock. 1866.
[2] Southwell Church, Nottingham. J. Place.

cemetery in nearly as sound a state as those of
recent burial. Stems of the old Scotch fir, too, which
have been dead a thousand years may be seen in
any number on the moist lands of Sutherlandshire,
the section of which presents all the appearance
and has all the odour of recent wood. The reason
of this is well known. Substances most prone to
decomposition are substances which contain nitrogen ; nitrogen hates combination and is always
trying to get out. Ligneous fibre contains little or
no nitrogen ; therefore, ligneous fibre, even under
conditions usually favourable to decomposition, is
nearly indestructible. I lay stress on this, because
it is not uncommonly supposed that wooden coffins
are readily perishable, and, therefore, unobjection-
able for the purposes of proper burial.

Nor, Sir, is there anything in my insistance on
a dissolution as speedy as may be of the buried
body to disturb the national sentiment which
prompts us to an exceptional treatment of the
bodies of the great. Princes, since they are few,
may still find rest in marble, and Great Men, since
they are fewer, among the shadows of our glorious
Abbey. All that is necessary in such cases is that
a certain period—a year or more—should be
allowed to elapse between the death and the final

entombment, during which time the body might lie embedded in charcoal, in a crypt to which the air has free ingress. A shrine of fine open metal work, such as that which surrounds the tomb of Henry VII. at Westminster, would answer admirably as the containing vessel for this charcoal, and the wicker coffin and its tenant (for in such cases coffins which are open on all sides must still be used) would lie unseen in the midst of it. On the anniversary of the death—supposing that to be the day selected for the final obsequies—this coffin, without being opened or its contents in any way disturbed, may be lifted out and transferred to its sepulchre. Its loss of weight will proclaim at once what has happened to the body within it. Except the bones, it will have disappeared. The charcoal, or rather the oxygen within its cells, will have done its work, and all that was perishable and vile of that body will have passed insensibly and inoffensively into the atmosphere.

(b) Considering that our reason for discontinuing intra-mural interment was that the soil of the old city graveyards had become so saturated and super-saturated with animal matter that it could no longer properly be called soil, it might be supposed that, in establishing the

new cemeteries, stringent provision would have been made that such a pollution of the ground should not again occur; the more so that it must have been foreseen that, by the inevitable extension of the town, the then suburban would become again the intra-mural cemetery, and that the horrors of the old graveyard would, thus, come to be repeated and multiplied. Not only was no such provision made, but one of the chief of the new companies gave prompt proof of its unfitness to comprehend and to use the powers entrusted to it by making the extraordinary proposal to bury 1,335,000 bodies in seven acres of ground. Here, Sir, since it may not else be believed, is this amazing proposal :—
"It has been found," say the newly-installed directors of the General Cemetery Company (Kensalgreen), in recommendation of the plans which they are proposing for their future guidance, "it has been found that seven acres will contain 133,500 graves ; each grave will contain ten coffins ; thus, accommodation will be found for 1,335,000 deceased paupers."[1] The very *naïveté* of this proposal might, one would think, have at once opened the eyes and excited the alarm of those who were conferring on these companies almost unlimited powers,

[1] Report, p. 8.

and have prepared them for the abuse of those powers which speedily followed. No such alarm, however, appears to have been excited, and a system of interment, founded we must suppose on this surprising calculation, was at once inaugurated and permitted. If, in the old graveyards, the Vestries and Guardians of the poor saved themselves expense by piling coffin upon coffin till the hole which they had dug would contain no more, the new Cemetery Companies increased their dividends and propitiated their shareholders by doing precisely the same thing. Here and there, indeed, by a sort of ingenious fiction, we find a few feet of ground sold in "perpetuity" to some one who, being dead and without heirs, has left no one to look after his property ; but in all material respects the new _régime_ differed in nothing from the old—the same prevention of resolution by the use of the closed coffin, the same pestiferous accumulation of unresolvable animal matter, and with it, of course, the same fevers to which they have given, and will yet, for many a day, give rise ; coffins air-tight only for as long as the nails in them remain unrusted and the lead which lines them resists the pressure of the dreadful gases within—thrust, as of old, into brick graves to become sooner or later filled with water, and huddled into cellars called catacombs, unceasing exhalants of every form of enteric disease—while the earth, the element capable of disposing of all this, and yet of retaining its own purity, by a refinement of ingenuity which can only be designated perverse, is prevented from exercising its function and condemned to become as putrid as the horrors it hides. Sir, if instead of writing to you, as I am doing, to urge a sane and simple compliance with a bountiful provision of Nature, I were writing to you to propose what we are now doing every day, and what the administrators of these cemeteries are persisting in doing against all remonstrance—namely, that we should collect together all the decaying residuum of this great city into boxes, and pile these boxes one above another in our open spaces and breathing places till these were filled with them, and then that we should do the same thing in great lines of circumvallation about the town till they, too, had to be enlarged by its extension, surely you would be warranted in treating me as a dangerous lunatic !

(c) Ignorant, then, as we have seen him to be of the nature of, and of the hygienic necessity for the resolution of the body after it has been buried in the earth, it is, perhaps, not surprising that the

Cemetery Director should choose a site for his speculation in a soil incapable of effecting that resolution, and that we should find him establishing his cemetery in the basin of the London clay, and in dangerous proximity to the town. But it is surprising that the Government, which refused to listen to the recommendations of the Board of Health in this matter, should have preferred to intrust the sanitary interests of a great city, and so important a duty as the burial of its dead, to a class of men who, however respectable, were actuated at best but by commercial motives, and who had shown themselves to be lamentably ignorant of the very first principles which should govern them in the management of such things.

(*d*) Again, apart from the improbability that a mere trading company would prove itself competent to deal with so large, so technical, and so delicate a question as the burial of the dead, it might have been foreseen that the material interests of such a company, its obligations to its shareholders, and its trade associations, could never be in harmony with, but must ever be opposed to, the interests of the public. One of the principal shareholders of these companies and most active attendants at their meetings is the undertaker, on whose patronage they mainly depend for their business, and who, under the threat of withdrawing his custom, may at any time virtually control their decisions.   Now, we know what the undertaker is, and how little his interests are our interests. But—the question occurs to me—do we know what the undertaker is? The undertaker is one who undertakes to do what another performs, and who engages to furnish what another supplies ; a free lance, who without a stock-in-trade or capital of his own, puts the words "furnishing undertaker" over his door, and carries on a profitable business, practically upon nothing—so profitable that for every dead body to be buried there are six others like him ready to undertake the burial of it. His real trade is that of an upholsterer, cabinetmaker, auctioneer, house-agent, tax-gatherer, builder, packing-case-maker, glover, hosier, or even publican.[1] We do not, of course, know this when we go to him, and, "place ourselves in his hands." How should we?   Nothing can be more sympathetic and decorous than his reception of us. He enters into our feelings as if they were his own, views things as we view them, deprecates what we

[1] Parliamentary Report on Extramural Sepulture, 1850, pp. 133, 134, 138.

deprecate, and—though he may insist upon the duty of doing the particular thing that we are about "handsomely"—cordially agrees with us on the impropriety of a needless expense and display ; so that when we have settled with him the cemetery to which we are to go (which is, of course, the cemetery with which he is connected), we take our leave, satisfied that we have fallen into good hands. As soon as we are gone, he places the whole of our affair in the hands of Messrs.——, the real furnishing undertakers, communicates his new stroke of business to the cemetery company in which he is interested (claiming his percentage upon it), and, except that he appears on the day of the funeral and sends us a bill very different in amount from that which the Messrs. —— will send him, washes his hands of us. Let me not be misunderstood ; I am not now describing the real undertaker, the respectable tradesman who has embarked his capital in the business, and who under our present circumstances is necessary to us, but a parasite class which interposes itself between him and the public, intercepts and takes his business out of his hands, and levies black mail both upon him and upon us. It is to this man and to his influence with the cemetery companies that we owe the maintenance of half the abuses of that part of the subject over which he more immediately presides. It was, for instance, unless I am much mistaken, not the Directors (properly speaking) of the Kensal-green Company who, only the other day, frustrated the intentions of Mr. Horsley when, in his preparation for the burial of a near relative, he "desired to obey in spirit and in letter the divine injunction to give earth to earth" by allowing the lid of the coffin to remain open—but the undertaker, who saw that it would never do to permit so dangerous an innovation as was contemplated. But, dismissing the undertaker (who, by the way, ought to be licensed), there is a part of this case which I will ask the chairman of the Kensal-green Company publicly to explain. In his letter to Mr. Horsley he informs him that the company are bound, by their Act, to refuse his request. On an examination of the Act, it would appear to contain no such disabling clause. Acts incorporating other cemeteries contain no such clause. Will he be good enough to point this one out to us? This is important—because the impression left by the chairman's letter on the public mind is that we are burying our dead improperly by Act of Parliament.

To insist at any length, after what has been said, on the necessity which exists for immediately closing the present cemeteries would be mere re-iteration. That they are full and more than full, that they will soon be as much a part of the town as the old graveyards, and that they have been formed in a soil incapable of resolving animal matter, are, in their aggregate, reasons more than sufficient to justify their immediate suppression. If it be urged that a portion of their ground remains unoccupied, and therefore that they are not "full," it may be answered that that portion which is occupied is so much too full that to add anything to such a mass of unresolved matter would be an unpardonable sanitary error. If it be pleaded that by the Acts of their incorporation they are forbidden to approach within a certain distance of habitable dwellings, and therefore that there is no need for their removal, it may be answered that there is nothing in those Acts which forbids the approach of those dwellings towards them. If it be advanced that a portion of the land in three out of eight of them is not exactly clay, it may be answered that all the other disabling conditions which affect these three affect them in such force as to warrant their

condemnation, without any consideration of that
palliative circumstance. In fine, on sanitary and
every other public ground, their maintenance as
burial-places is no longer admissible. And surely,
Sir, on the ground that it is neither to the interest
nor the dignity of a great nation to intrust the
burial of its dead to speculative associations—
ignorant of their duties as we have seen them to
be, and animated by no higher impulses than such
as arise out of a spirit of trade—it is also inadmis-
sible. If the Burial of the Dead, in short, may
not unreasonably be compared in importance with
the main drainage, is it not at least as fit—would
it not be much fitter—that so serious a trust
should be undertaken either by the Board of
Works, or by a special department under its
immediate supervision ?

5. What, then, are the considerations which
should influence us in the choice of ground for
a new cemetery ? The soil should be of a nature
to favour the resolution of the body within a
certain time—say in from three to seven years.
The cemetery to be established should be to
the east of the town, because it is the east end
which is most densely populated, and by a class
to whom distance and expense of transit are

of importance; because it should be seaward
rather than landward, and subject to the visita-
tion of large bodies of movable air, and because
prevalent winds should blow from the town towards it, and not from it towards the town;
because, as the whole stream of mortality
would be constantly directed towards it, access
to it should be, not by narrow road but by broad
river, progress by which is silent, inexpensive, and
of a nature not to interfere with the living traffic
of the town; because the physical conditions
of the whole region east of London are favourable
to its formation and to plantation, and peculiarly
unfavourable to the increase of population; and,
finally, because the presence of a large well-
planted cemetery there, instead of being a detri-
ment to such a region, would (for reasons which
I have already advanced and which I must venture to adhere to), be a benefit to it.

These, then, being the conditions essential to
the formation of any new cemetery, everything
would seem to point either to the low lands on
the Essex bank of the river about Rainham, Pur-
fleet, and Grays, or to the higher lands of the
Kentish bank, east of Erith, as singularly favourable to the purpose. On the Essex side the soil

is alluvial, the subsoil chalky, and the general surface flat. On the Kentish side the soil is for the most part chalky and the surface broken and uneven. The preponderance of advantages would therefore appear, should the soil prove deep enough, to lie on the Essex side. As to the acreage required for the purpose of burying the whole mortality of London on the principle of giving a separate grave to each body, and of allowing it an undisturbed tenure of that grave for ten years—that is to say, for a longer time than would be necessary for its dissolution—a thousand acres would bury 100,000 bodies a year for ever; therefore, allowing for the increase of population to be expected with lapse of time, and adopting, say, 200,000 as a probable mean of the prospective annual mortality of Greater London, a total of 2,000 acres of cemetery space, once obtained, would, *without entailing upon us any further outlay at any future time, bury the whole of this mortality for ever.* A thousand acres of that space already exist at Woking, so that the operation I am supposing contemplates the purchase of the present suburban cemeteries (500 acres), and the acquisition of 1,000 acres in the region I have indicated. In negotiating with the present

cemeteries, account would, of course, be taken of
the sales they have already effected "in perpetuity,"
and of the very little land, available for any useful
purposes whatever, that they have yet to sell.
Meanwhile we have, as I have said, at Woking a
thousand acres of excellent land for all the purposes of a cemetery, and capable, *upon the primary
condition I insist upon of insuring the resolution of
the body*, of effecting 100,000 interments per annum
for ever, the Act of Incorporation of that cemetery
providing also a separate grave for each body, and
containing no disabling clause against the practice
of interments upon the principles I am advocating.
The Woking Cemetery is also the only existing
cemetery in which the burial of a body can be
effected with the present certainty that it will not
be disturbed for ten years. In the absence, therefore, of any ameliorations whatever of our present
cemeterial system being obtainable, it is plainly
to the interest of every class, high and low, to
avoid the seething suburban cemeteries and to
bury their dead at Woking.

And now, Sir, as I turn over the last page with
which I shall have to trouble you, I would gladly
know how far I have succeeded in conveying to
others my own sense of the gravity of the situa-

tion we have created; whether the reader will have been able to realize, from what I have said, the certain effect on the life and health of this and of future generations of the mass of festering corruption which we have been laying up and cannot now get rid of—unless, indeed, we deal with it as we did in Holborn; whether he is conscious that for a time to come, at least equal to that during which we have been creating this evil, the soil which we have been so industriously sowing with disease and death must continue to yield its annual harvest; whether he will remember that as long as these horrible coffins hold together, the plague to which we have given existence cannot be stayed, and that we must wait their disintegration and the resolution of their contents before we can hope for the life-prolonging effect of a pure soil, pure water, and a pure atmosphere.

I am, Sir, your obedient servant,

F. SEYMOUR HADEN.

June 16, 1875.

P.S.—Since, from the publicity which has been given to the suggestion of the wicker coffin, it may be supposed that I look upon its adoption as an essential part of my scheme, it may be well to repeat here what I have said at pp. 51, 52—namely, that I attach no more importance to it than I should to *any other agency by which the principles I have advocated might with equal efficiency be carried out.*

THE END.

LONDON: R. CLAY, SONS, AND TAYLOR, PRINTERS.